Ulrich Renz / Barbara Brinkmann

İyi uykular, küçük kurt

Schlaf gut, kleiner Wolf

İki dilli resimli bir kitap

Çeviri:

Şerife Aydoğmuş (Türkçe)

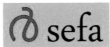

Download audiobook at:

www.sefa-bilingual.com/mp3

Password for free access:

Türkçe: **henüz mevcut değil sesli kitap**

Almanca: **LWDE1314**

"İyi geceler Tim, yarın aramaya devam ederiz.
Şimdi güzelce uyu!"

„Gute Nacht, Tim! Wir suchen morgen weiter.
Jetzt schlaf schön!"

Hava karardı.

Draußen ist es schon dunkel.

Peki Tim ne yapıyor?

Was macht Tim denn da?

Dışarı çıkıyor, parka gidiyor.

Orda aradığı nedir?

Er geht raus, zum Spielplatz.

Was sucht er da?

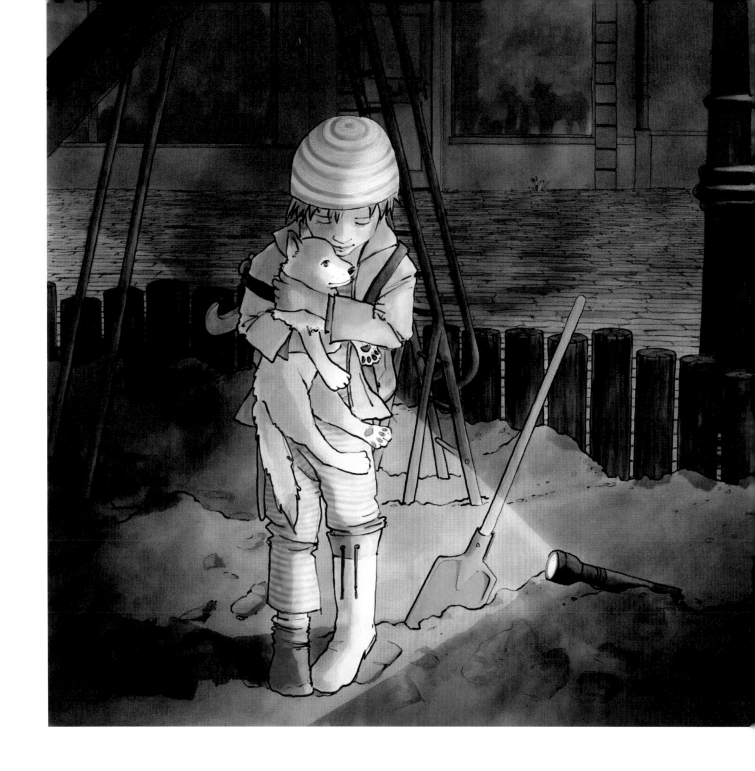

Küçük peluş kurdu!

Onsuz uyuyamıyor.

Den kleinen Wolf!

Ohne den kann er nicht schlafen.

Kimdir şurdan gelen?

Wer kommt denn da?

Marie!

O da topunu arıyor.

Marie!

Die sucht ihren Ball.

Tobi ne arıyor peki?

Und was sucht Tobi?

Vinçini.

Seinen Bagger.

Peki Nala ne arıyor?

Und was sucht Nala?

Bebeğini.

Ihre Puppe.

Çoçukların yatağa gitmeleri gerekmiyor mu?

Kedi çok şaşırıyor.

Müssen die Kinder nicht ins Bett?

Die Katze wundert sich sehr.

Şimdi kim geliyor?

Wer kommt denn jetzt?

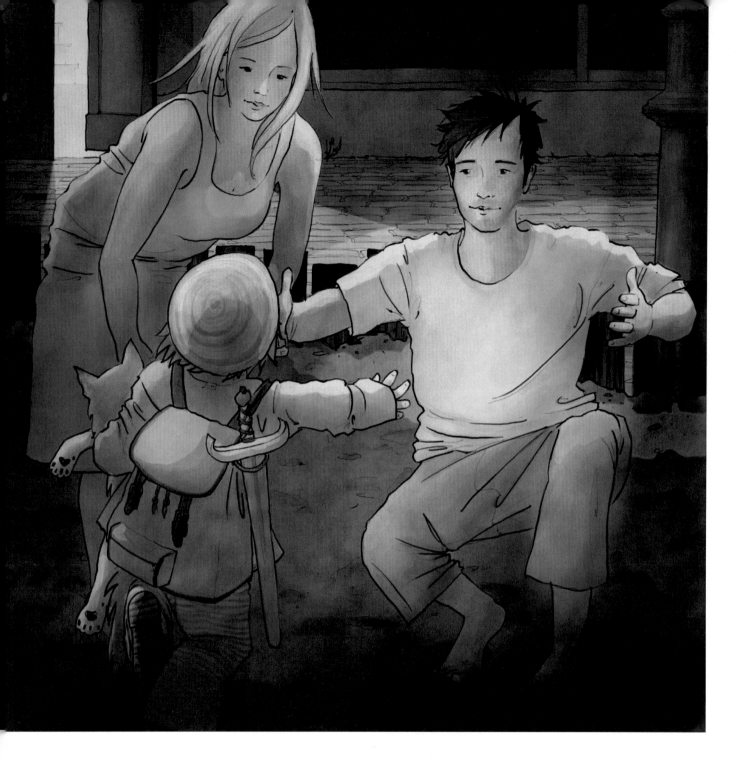

Tim'in Annesi ve Babası!

Tim olmadan uyuyamıyorlar.

Die Mama und der Papa von Tim!

Ohne ihren Tim können sie nicht schlafen.

Bir çok kişi daha geliyor! Marie'nin Babası.
Tobi'nin Dedesi. Ve Nala'nın Annesi.

Und da kommen noch mehr! Der Papa von Marie. Der
Opa von Tobi. Und die Mama von Nala.

Hadi ama çabuk yatağa!

Jetzt aber schnell ins Bett!

"İyi geceler, Tim!
Sabahleyin aramak zorunda değiliz artık."

„Gute Nacht, Tim!
Morgen müssen wir nicht mehr suchen."

İyi uykular, küçük kurt!

„Schlaf gut, kleiner Wolf!"

More about me ...

Que duermas bien, pequeño lobo
Schlaf gut, kleiner Wolf
Ulrich Renz / Barbara Brinkmann
español · bilingüe · alemán

Schlaf gut, kleiner Wolf
راحت بخواب، گرگ کوچک
Ulrich Renz / Barbara Brinkmann
Deutsch · bilingual · Persisch (Farsi)

Dors bien, petit loup
Sleep Tight, Little Wolf
Ulrich Renz / Barbara Brinkmann
français · bilingue · anglais

نم جيدا أيها الذئب الصغير
Sov gott, lilla vargen
Ulrich Renz / Barbara Brinkmann
العربية · شائی اللغة · السويدية

Sofðu rótt, litli úlfur
Όνειρα γλυκά, μικρέ λύκε
Ulrich Renz / Barbara Brinkmann
Íslenska · tvímála · gríska

Dorme bem, lobinho
Suaviter dormi, lupe parve
Ulrich Renz / Barbara Brinkmann
português · bilingue · latino

Schlaf gut, kleiner Wolf
おおかみくんも
くっすり　おやすみなさい
Ulrich Renz / Barbara Brinkmann
Deutsch · bilingual · Japanisch

잘 자, 꼬마 늑대야
Slaap lekker, kleine wolf
Ulrich Renz / Barbara Brinkmann
한국어 · 양국어 · 네덜란드어

Приятных снов, маленький волчёнок
Sleep Tight, Little Wolf
Ulrich Renz / Barbara Brinkmann
русский · двуязычный · английский

راحت بخواب، گرگ کوچک
Schlaf gut, kleiner Wolf
Ulrich Renz / Barbara Brinkmann
فارسی · دوزبانی · آلمانی

Que duermas bien, pequeño lobo
نم جيداً أيها الذئبُ الصغير
Ulrich Renz / Barbara Brinkmann
español · bilingüe · árabe

സുഖമായി ഉറങ്ങൂ
ചെന്നായി കുഞ്ഞേ
Dormi bene, piccolo lupo
Ulrich Renz / Barbara Brinkmann
മലയാളം · ദ്വിഭാഷ · ഇറ്റാലിയൻ

Dormi bene, piccolo lupo
जम के सोना , छोटे भेड़िये
Ulrich Renz / Barbara Brinkmann
italiano · bilinguale · hindi

ፁበቅ ድቃስ፥ ጎኣሸቶይ ተኹኣ
Selamat tidur, si serigala
Ulrich Renz / Barbara Brinkmann
ትግ · ብ ኽዕ ቆኛ · Malaysian

Śpij dobrze, mały wilku
ძილო ნებისა, პაწარა მგელო
Ulrich Renz / Barbara Brinkmann
polski · Dwujęzyczna · gruziński

Солодких снів, маленький вовчику
잘 자, 꼬마 늑대야
Ulrich Renz / Barbara Brinkmann
українська · двомовний · корейська

Children's Books for the Global Village

Ever more children are born away from their parents' home countries, and are balancing between the languages of their mother, their father, their grandparents, and their peers. Our bilingual books are meant to help bridge the language divides that cross more and more families, neighborhoods and kindergartens in the globalized world.

Little Wolf also proposes:

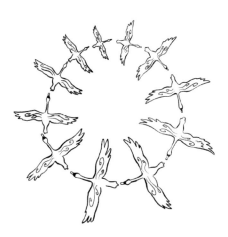

The Wild Swans

Bilingual picture book
adapted from
a fairy tale by
Hans Christian Andersen

▶ Reading age 4 and up

www.childrens-books-bilingual.com

NEW! Little Wolf in Sign Language

Home	Authors	Little Wolf	About

Bilingual Children's Books - in any language you want

Welcome to Little Wolf's Language Wizard!

Just choose the two languages in which you want to read to your children:

Language 1:

French

Language 2:

Icelandic

Go!

Learn more about our bilingual books at www.childrens-books-bilingual.com. At the heart of this website you will find what we call our "Language Wizard". It contains more than 60 languages and any of their bilingual combinations: Just select, in a simple drop-down-menu, the two languages in which you'd like to read "Little Wolf" or "The Wild Swans" to your child – and the book is instantly made available, ready for order as an ebook download or as a printed edition.

As time goes by ...

... the little ones grow older, and start to read on their own. Here is Little Wolf's recommendation to them:

BO & FRIENDS

Smart detective stories for smart children

Reading age: 10 + - www.bo-and-friends.com

Wie die Zeit vergeht ...

Irgendwann sind aus den süßen Kleinen süße Große geworden

– die jetzt sogar selber lesen können. Der kleine Wolf empfiehlt:

MOTTE & CO

Kinderkrimis zum Mitdenken

Lesealter ab 10 – www.motte-und-co.de

About the authors

Ulrich Renz was born in Stuttgart, Germany, in 1960. After studying French literature in Paris he graduated from medical school in Lübeck and worked as head of a scientific publishing company. He is now a writer of non-fiction books as well as children's fiction books. – www.ulrichrenz.de

Barbara Brinkmann was born in Munich, Germany, in 1969. She grew up in the foothills of the Alps and studied architecture and medicine for a while in Munich. She now works as a freelance graphic artist, illustrator and writer. – www.bcbrinkmann.com

© 2018 by Sefa Verlag Kirsten Bödeker, Lübeck, Germany
www.sefa-verlag.de

IT: Paul Bödeker, München, Germany
Font: Noto Sans

ISBN: 9783739945125

Version: 20180225

47085810R00015

Made in the USA
Columbia, SC
28 December 2018